Excel From Beginner to Master
5-Days Crash Course.

Learn Excel Quickly
with Step-by-Steps Examples and
Secret Tricks

Riley Cobb

Table of content

Chapter 1: Introduction to Excel

- What is Excel and why is it important?

Excel is a powerful spreadsheet tool made by Microsoft that is used for data management, analysis, and visualization. It has grown to be one of the most widely used business apps and is now a vital tool for professionals in a variety of fields, including engineering, marketing, and finance.

Excel's fundamental building block is a grid of cells that may be used to store and manage data. Each cell in the spreadsheet can have a value, text, or a formula that computes anything based on values in other cells. The information can then be arranged into tables, charts, and graphs to reveal important details about the underlying data.

Excel's adaptability is one of its primary advantages. It can be used for a variety of purposes, from straightforward math to intricate financial modeling. Excel can be used to design a cash flow model that predicts future revenue and expenses, or a small business owner may use it to make a budget spreadsheet that tracks income and expenses. Excel may also be used to build interactive dashboards that offer current information on a company's or organization's key performance indicators (KPIs).

Excel's capacity to automate tedious processes is another key feature. Users may easily do computations on massive volumes of data without the need for human input by using formulae and functions. The use of macros, which are brief programs that automate actions inside of Excel, is also supported. Users' productivity can increase and a lot of time can be saved by doing this.

The extensive formatting choices in Excel enable users to produce spreadsheets and reports with a professional appearance. Users can alter the design of cells, tables, charts, and graphs to suit their own requirements, and they can even make their own templates that can be used to new projects in the future.

Excel is a crucial tool for cooperation and communication in addition to its adaptability, automation, and customization choices. It offers a variety of capabilities for recording changes, making comments, and securing sensitive data in addition to enabling users to share spreadsheets and workbooks with others.

For everyone who wants to organize, analyze, and visualize data, Excel is an indispensable tool because of its strength and versatility. Excel is a useful tool that may assist you in improving your decision-making, saving time, and increasing your productivity, whether you are a small business owner, financial analyst, or marketing expert.

- Navigating the Excel interface

Anyone who wants to use Excel effectively must be able to navigate the application's interface. The Excel interface is divided into multiple significant sections, each with a distinct purpose. If users know how to explore these areas, they can quickly and simply find the tools and capabilities they need to interact with data.

The Ribbon, which is located at the top of the screen, serves as the focal point of the Excel interface. The Ribbon is broken up into tabs, each of which is intended for a specific job type. For instance, the Home tab has tools for text and number formatting, while the Insert tab has tools for adding graphs, tables, and other objects to a spreadsheet.

Each tab has groups of related tools that can be accessed by clicking on the corresponding icon. In contrast to the Number group, which has tools for formatting numbers as currency, percentages, or dates, the Font group in the Home tab has tools for changing font size, style, and color.

In addition to the Ribbon, Excel has a number of other significant areas that are used to traverse the interface. A toolbar that may be configured to add shortcuts to frequently performed operations is called the Quick Access Toolbar. It can be moved if necessary, however by default it is located above the Ribbon.

The Formula Bar is yet another essential component of the Excel interface. It is located above the worksheet area and shows what is presently being selected in the cell. The Formula Bar allows users to quickly add formulas, text, or numbers and change the contents of a cell.

At the bottom of the screen, in the Status Bar, is information about how the spreadsheet is currently functioning. It displays the total number of chosen cells, the current cell reference, and other helpful data.

In the worksheet area, users enter and modify data. A grid of cells that can store text, numbers, or formulas makes up the document. The worksheet's scroll bars and cell-browsing tools can be used by users to navigate the worksheet.

Anyone who wishes to use Excel to its full potential must be able to navigate the user interface. If users are aware of the various areas of the interface and how to use them, they may quickly and simply get the tools and capabilities they require to engage with data. Learning how to utilize the Excel interface is essential whether you are a new or experienced user who wants to take full advantage of this incredible program.

- Creating a new workbook

Starting an Excel workbook is the first step in using the program. Workbooks are collections of spreadsheets that can be used for many different things, such as project planning, data management, and financial analysis. Excel gives you the option of starting from scratch or using a pre-made template to create a new worksheet.

To create a new workbook, open Excel and choose "Blank workbook" from the menu on the home screen. This will open a brand-new workbook with a single blank page. Then, using Excel's many features and capabilities, you may start entering data, formatting cells, and performing calculations.

As an alternative, you can use one of the many pre-made Excel templates to create a new worksheet. Some of the uses for which templates are made include billing, project management, and budgeting. You can use a template by selecting the relevant template category by clicking the "New" button on the home screen. The template that best suits your needs can then be selected from a number of templates that Excel will present to you.

A new worksheet can have data added to it after it has been made. Data can be entered into cells in Excel, and the cells can be set up to display the data in a variety of ways. For example, you can format cells to show decimal points, dates, or currency symbols. To do operations like addition, subtraction, multiplication, and division, you can also add formulas to cells. Excel's built-in functions can be used to do intricate calculations for tasks like statistical analysis and financial modeling.

You can incorporate graphs, charts, and other visuals into your workbook using Excel. These can be used to display data in a format that is comprehensible and interpreted. You may modify the appearance of a number of chart types in Excel, including pie charts, bar charts, and line charts.

Excel offers a number of tools in addition to these capabilities that can help you manage your worksheet better. You may easily find and replace certain data in your spreadsheet by using the "Find and Change" tool, for example. The "Sort" and

"Filter" tools can also be used to arrange and streamline your data analysis.

The creation of a new worksheet is an essential first step in the Excel work process. Starting with a blank page allows you to tailor your workbook to your specific needs and make the most of Excel's powerful capabilities to successfully manage and analyze your data. You can master Excel and create visually appealing and useful worksheets with time and practice.

- Entering data into cells

Data entry into cells is one of the key skills an Excel user has to acquire. In Excel, you may enter a variety of different types of data into cells, including text, numbers, and dates. By knowing how to precisely insert data into cells, users may create precise and helpful spreadsheets that help them finish their work.

To enter data, merely click the cell and start typing. The data will be displayed in the cell, and the Formula Bar will also display it. Users may enter any type of data, including text, numbers, and dates. Excel will automatically format the data based on the kind it detects.

Text entered into a cell by a user can contain any combination of characters, numbers, and symbols. Excel supports a wide range of font sizes and styles, and users can format the text by selecting options like bold, italic, and underline. By using the Alignment group on the Home tab, users can easily relocate and align the text within a cell.

When entering numbers into a cell, users are free to use any combination of digits, decimal points, and mathematical operators. Excel supports a wide range of number formats, including currency, percentage, and scientific notation. The Amount group in the Home tab also allows users to change the number of displayed decimal places and apply formatting options.

When entering dates into cells, users can type them in a variety of formats, including month/day/year or day/month/year. Excel will immediately recognize the data as a date and format it accordingly. Users can choose different formatting options and change how the date is shown by using the Date group on the Home tab.

In Excel, calculations can be performed on data entered into cells using formulas and functions. Before entering cell references, mathematical operators, or functions to put a formula into a cell, users must start formulations with an equal sign (=). Excel will automatically calculate the formula's result and display it in the cell.

The ability to enter data into cells in Excel is a fundamental skill that every user should possess. By knowing how to enter text, numbers, and dates correctly, users may create accurate spreadsheets that help them finish their duties. Since it supports formulae and functions and enables users to perform complex calculations on their data, Excel is an essential tool for professionals in a range of industries.

Chapter 2: Basic Formulas and Functions

- Understanding formulas and functions

Formulas and functions make up the core of Excel. They give you the ability to carry out complex computations and handle data in a way that is not possible with human approaches. To get the most of Excel's capabilities, you must thoroughly understand formulae and functions.

In Excel, a formula is an equation that performs calculations on one or more integers. Simple arithmetic to intricate statistical analysis can be performed using formulas that be input into cells. In Excel, formulas always start with the equals sign (=), then the desired computation.

Use the expression "=A1+B1" to combine the values in cells A1 and B1, for instance. The calculation would then be carried out by Excel, and the outcome would be shown in the formula cell.

On the other hand, functions are pre-programmed formulas that carry out specific calculations. Numerous tasks can be performed using Excel's built-in functions, such as financial analysis, date and time calculations, and statistical analysis. Start by entering the function name into a cell, followed be an open parenthesis, to use a function in Excel. The function arguments are then entered, separated by commas, and the parenthesis are closed. Use the "AVERAGE" function, for instance, to determine the average of a group of cells. To utilize this function, you would type "=AVERAGE(A1:A10)" into a different cell. The average value of cells A1 through A10 would then be calculated by Excel, and the result would be shown in the formula cell.

There are numerous functions in Excel that can be used for a wide range of tasks. Some of the most often used functions include SUM, AVERAGE, MAX, MIN, COUNT, and IF. Simple calculations like adding a range of integers or counting the number of cells that satisfy a particular criterion can be performed using these functions, as well as more complex calculations like statistical analysis and financial modeling. If you want to understand Excel, learning how to apply formulae and functions is essential. Understanding these tools will enable you to handle data and do complex calculations in ways that manual approaches cannot. With practice and expertise, you may master the use of formulas and functions and create workbooks that are both practical and aesthetically pleasing.

- Basic arithmetic operations

One of Excel's most essential functions is its ability to execute simple arithmetic operations on data entered into cells, enabling users to make mathematical computations. Numerous arithmetic operations, including addition, subtraction, multiplication, and division, are supported by Excel. Users can create precise and effective spreadsheets that help them fulfill their duties by knowing how to apply these methods effectively.

Simple arithmetic operations can be carried out in Excel by employing the mathematical operators plus (+), minus (-), asterisk (*), and slash (/). Users can enter the first number in one cell and the second number in another cell, for example, and then use the plus operator to join the two cells to add the two numbers. Excel will compute the outcome automatically and display it in the cell.

Additionally, users can quickly add many cells together by using the Sum function. Select the relevant range of cells, then click the AutoSum button on the Home tab to use the Sum function. The Sum function will be inserted by Excel, and the specified cells' sum will be computed.

Subtraction uses the minus operator, much like addition (-). Users can enter the initial number into one cell and the second number into another cell, followed by the minus operator, to subtract one number from another. Excel will compute the outcome automatically and display it in the cell.

Division and multiplication are also crucial arithmetic operations in Excel. By placing the first number in one cell and the second number in another cell, followed by the asterisk operator, users can multiply two numbers. Users can enter the first number in one cell and the second number in another cell to divide one number by another. Then, they can use the slash operator to divide the first cell by the second cell. Excel will compute the outcome automatically and display it in the cell. In addition to these basic arithmetic operations, Excel also supports a sizable number of complicated mathematical operations, such as square roots, logarithms, and trigonometric functions. These functions can be used to do more complex calculations on data entered in cells and are available via the Formulas tab.

Excel's core arithmetic operations enable users to conduct mathematical calculations on data entered in cells. By learning how to correctly apply these processes, users are able to construct accurate and efficient spreadsheets that assist them in completing their responsibilities. Excel's support for sophisticated mathematical functions also makes it a potent tool for experts in a variety of industries.

- Using functions like SUM, AVERAGE, and MAX

Three of the most frequently used Excel functions are SUM, AVERAGE, and MAX. You can quickly and easily do basic calculations on large data sets with these methods.

A range of cells can be added using the SUM function in Excel. Select the cells you want to add, then type "=SUM(A1:A10)" in another cell to use the SUM function. The sum of the values in cells A1 through A10 will then be computed and shown by Excel in the cell with the formula.

The average value of numerous cells is calculated using the AVERAGE function. To use the AVERAGE function, type the following into a different cell: "=AVERAGE(A1:A10)". The average value of cells A1 through A10 will then be calculated and shown in the formula cell by Excel.

The MAX function is used to find the highest value contained within a cell range. In a another cell, type "=MAX(A1:A10)" to use the MAX function. The cell containing the formula will show the outcome.

Numerous calculations can be made using these Excel tools. For instance, you may use the AVERAGE function to determine the average value of a set of data or the SUM function to add up the values in a column of numbers. The MAX function can be used to determine the data set with the highest value or the salesperson with the best performance. Excel contains a number of advanced functions that can be used to carry out more complex calculations in addition to these basic operations. For instance, conditional calculations depending on given circumstances can be carried out using the IF function. Depending on a specified value, the VLOOKUP function can be used to get data from a table. To count the number of cells in a specified range that meet a specific criteria, use the COUNTIF function.

You can quickly and simply perform calculations on large data sets by being familiar with methods like SUM, AVERAGE, and

MAX. These functions can be combined with other functions and formulas to perform a variety of data manipulations and more complex calculations. You can master Excel operations with practice and expertise and create worksheets that are both aesthetically beautiful and useful.

- Relative vs. absolute cell references

Relative and absolute cell references are two essential ideas that Excel users can utilize to perform calculations on data entered into cells. By knowing the difference between relative and absolute cell references, users can create more complex formulas and functions that accurately reflect the data they are working with.

In Excel, a relative cell reference is the standard reference type. When a formula or function is transferred to a new cell, the references to the cells in the original formula or function are changed to point to the new position of the formula or function. If, for example, a formula in cell A1 refers to cell B1 and the formula is transferred to cell A2, the cell reference in the formula will shift right away to cell B2. This is true because the reference is based on the location of the formula rather than the location of the original cell.

On the other hand, when a formula or function is copied to a different cell, an absolute cell reference remains the same. A cell reference is considered absolute if the dollar sign ($) appears before the column letter and row number. If a formula in cell A1 refers to cell B1 and the formula is moved to cell A2, for example, the cell reference in the formula will always be B1, regardless of where the formula is situated.

An absolute cell reference can be used to refer to a fixed cell or set of fixed cells in a formula or function. If a user needs to compute a percentage based on a fixed number, such as a tax rate, they can, for example, use an absolute cell reference to ensure that the tax rate is always used in the computation. This is especially useful when working with huge datasets or complex formulas that call for precise computations.

A mixed cell reference is another reference type that includes absolute and relative references. Users can set a cell reference's row or column to be fixed while allowing the other to change depending on where the formula or function resides. To denote a reference to a mixed cell, the dollar sign ($) must be before either the column letter or the row number, but not both. If a formula in cell A1 refers to cell $B2 and the formula is transferred to cell A2, the cell reference in the formula will change to $B3. This is because the row reference is local to the position of the formula but the column reference is fixed.

Understanding the difference between relative and absolute cell references is a crucial skill for Excel users who frequently work with complex formulae and functions. By choosing the proper type of reference when dealing with large datasets, users can shorten their workday and become more productive while also ensuring that their calculations accurately reflect the data they are using.

Chapter 3: Data Analysis with Tables and Charts

- Creating tables to organize data

Excel's ability to construct tables is a practical tool that enables users to arrange and examine huge amounts of data. Tables offer a structured style for data entry, making it simpler for users to sort, filter, and analyze their data. By understanding how to create tables in Excel, users can increase their productivity and gain deeper insights into their data.

Users must first decide which data will be included in the table before they can begin building one in Excel. By dragging the mouse over the cells that contain data, this is achieved. Users can click the Table button on the Insert tab after choosing their data. When a cell range is selected, Excel will recognize it and ask the user to confirm their selection.

Once a table has been built, users can modify its appearance and features using the Table Tools Design tab. Tools for formatting the table, adding and deleting columns and rows, as well as applying filters and sorting options, are available on this page. The Table Styles group allows users to apply a pre-designed style to the table, which can help the table look better and be simpler to interpret.

One of the main advantages of using tables in Excel is the ability to sort and filter data. Users can choose whether to sort the data in a table in ascending or descending order by clicking on the column heading. Additionally, users can sort the data at several levels, which is useful when working with sizable datasets.

Another helpful technique for reducing data to certain criteria is to filter the data in a table. By selecting the Filter button on the Table Tools Design tab, filters may be applied to data. A drop-down window will appear where users can select specific filtering criteria for the data. Users can also utilize the table's search box to look up specific data.

The capacity to perform calculations on the data is another advantage of using Excel tables. Users can add summary calculations to the table, such as sums or averages, by using the Total Row functionality. On the Table Tools Design tab, check the Total Row box. Next, choose the calculation style. For Excel users who need to organize and analyze massive amounts of data, the ability to create tables is crucial. By employing tables, users can increase their productivity, gain deeper insights into their data, and base their decisions more intelligently on the information at hand. Excel is a useful tool for experts in a variety of industries since it can sort, filter, and calculate data within tables.

- Sorting and filtering table data

With Excel's advanced sorting and filtering features, users can rapidly and efficiently organize and analyze huge amounts of data. Users can arrange data in a table's columns in either ascending or descending order by sorting the data. Users can limit the data in a table by filtering it according to predefined criteria, such as text, numbers, dates, and custom criteria. Understanding how to sort and filter table data can help Excel users better comprehend their data and make more informed decisions.

By clicking on the relevant column's heading, users can sort table data in the appropriate order. Excel will automatically sort the data in ascending order based on this column. By clicking the column heading a second time, users can sort the data in decreasing order. Users can quickly sort the data based on multiple columns by clicking the Sort button on the Table Tools Design tab and choosing the columns to sort by. An additional powerful tool that lets users restrict data based on certain criteria is filtering data in a table. Users can apply a filter to a table by clicking the Filter button on the Table Tools Design tab. As a result, a drop-down menu will appear where users can select specific data filtering criteria. Users can also use the Search box to locate particular data in the table. Excel's filtering tool enables users to apply numerous filters to a table, which is especially helpful when working with huge datasets. Users can apply filters to several columns and utilize a combination of text, numeric, and date filters to refine the data. The Custom Filter option allows users to design complicated filters based on specified criteria.

Excel has advanced filtering tools that allow users to design more complex filters in addition to basic filtering. The advanced filtering options allow for the creation of filters based on numerous criteria, the use of wildcards to search for specific data, and the filtering of data that meets specified circumstances.

One of the primary benefits of sorting and filtering table data is the capacity to evaluate vast amounts of data fast and efficiently. Users can uncover patterns, trends, and outliers that may not be immediately obvious by sorting and filtering the data. This can be very helpful when working with complex datasets or attempting to locate specific data points.

Sorting and filtering table data is a potent Excel tool that enables users to efficiently organize and analyze vast amounts of data. Excel's ability for sorting, filtering, and advanced filtering capabilities makes it a potent tool for professionals in a variety of industries. By understanding how to sort and filter table data in Excel, users can obtain a greater grasp of their data and make more informed decisions based on the available information.

- Creating basic charts (e.g. bar, line, pie)

The ability to make basic charts in Excel is a handy feature that may be utilized to aid in data visualization. In addition to other chart types, Excel has bar charts, line charts, and pie charts that can all be quickly and easily created.

A bar chart is a diagram that uses bars to represent data. Before you can create a bar chart in Excel, you must first decide the data you want to chart. After selecting your data, select the "Insert" tab and the "Bar" chart type. After that, Excel will generate a simple bar chart that you may customize. A line chart is one that uses lines to display the data. To create a line chart in Excel, choose the data you want to display and click the "Insert" button once again. This time, you select the "Line" chart type. Next, Excel creates a basic line chart that can be modified by adding titles, labels, and legends.

A pie chart is a visual representation of data in the form of pie slices. To make a pie chart in Excel, choose the data you want to visualize, then select the "Insert" tab. This time, you select the "Pie" chart type. Next, Excel constructs a basic pie chart that may be modified by adding legends and labels.

You can further modify your chart once you've created it by changing the font styles, font sizes, and other formatting options. You may also include titles, labels, and legends to make your chart simpler to understand.

The charts in Excel are a powerful tool that may be used to convey information and support data visualization. By creating straightforward charts like bar charts, line charts, and pie charts, you may quickly and easily show data in an intelligible way. With effort and expertise, you may become a master at creating and customizing charts in Excel and create workbooks that are both functional and aesthetically pleasing.

Chapter 4: Advanced Formulas and Functions

- Conditional statements (IF, AND, OR)

Conditional statements are a valuable Excel feature that allows users to conduct computations based on certain circumstances. In Excel, the most common conditional statements are IF, AND, and OR. Users can develop more sophisticated formulas and functions that appropriately reflect the data they are working with if they understand how to apply these statements.

In Excel, the IF statement is used to conduct a computation based on a specific condition. The IF statement is divided into three sections: a logical test, a value if true, and a value if false. The logical test is a statement that can be true or false. If the logical test is true, Excel returns the value specified in the value if true parameter. If the logical test fails, Excel returns the value specified in the value if false argument.

In Excel, the AND statement is used to make a computation based on numerous conditions. If all criteria are true, the AND statement returns true; otherwise, it returns false. To generate more complex calculations based on numerous circumstances, utilize the AND statement in conjunction with the IF statement.

The Excel OR statement is used to calculate based on many variables. If any of the requirements are met, the OR statement returns true; otherwise, it returns false. Use the OR statement along with the IF statement to produce computations that are more sophisticated and are based on multiple factors.

Excel gives users the option to create more complex computations based on a variety of conditions by offering nested IF statements in addition to the traditional IF, AND, and OR expressions. Nested IF statements are nested IF statements that can be used in a hierarchical manner to carry out calculations based on various conditions.

Conditional formatting, which enables users to highlight specific cells based on specific conditions, is another helpful Excel feature. Cells that fulfill certain criteria, such as being greater than or less than a particular value or containing a specific text or value, can be highlighted using conditional formatting. This can be quite useful when working with large datasets because it enables users to quickly and simply discover certain data points.

In general, conditional statements are a crucial part of Excel since they let users perform calculations based on certain criteria. Employing IF, AND, and OR statements as well as nested IF statements allows users to create more complex formulas and functions that accurately reflect the data they are working with. Excel is a useful tool for professionals working in a variety of disciplines because it has conditional formatting capabilities.

- Lookup functions (VLOOKUP, HLOOKUP, INDEX/MATCH)

The ability to use lookup functions to search for specific data in a table or range of cells is a crucial Excel feature. The Excel lookup functions VLOOKUP, HLOOKUP, and INDEX/MATCH can be used to perform a variety of lookup tasks.

The VLOOKUP function searches the leftmost column of a table for a particular value and then returns a corresponding value from another column. When using the VLOOKUP function, you must specify the value you want to look up, the cell range in which the table is contained, the column number where the value you want to retrieve is located, and whether you want an exact or approximate match. For instance, you could use the VLOOKUP function to verify the pricing of a specific item in a product database.

Unlike the VLOOKUP function, the HLOOKUP function searches the top row of a table for a certain value and returns a corresponding value from that row. When using the

HLOOKUP function, you must specify the value you want to look up, the cell range in which the table is contained, the row number in which the value you want to retrieve is situated, and whether you want an exact or approximate match. For instance, you could use the HLOOKUP function to look up the sales figures for a specific month in a sales table.

The more flexible INDEX/MATCH function can be used to search for a certain value in a table or range of cells; it will then return a value from a different column or row. While the INDEX function retrieves a value from a particular row or column in a table, the MATCH function locates the location of a given value within a range of cells. Together, these tools are capable of handling complex lookup jobs that the VLOOKUP and HLOOKUP routines are unable to.

Lookup functions are a key Excel feature that allow you to locate and get specific data from a table or group of cells. By mastering lookup functions like VLOOKUP, HLOOKUP, and INDEX/MATCH, you can complete challenging lookup tasks quickly and efficiently. You may become an expert user of

Excel's lookup functions and create worksheets that are both aesthetically beautiful and useful with practice.

- Text functions (CONCATENATE, LEFT, RIGHT)

Text functions are an essential component of Excel that enable users to modify text data in a variety of ways. Text functions are a collection of formulas that can be used to do a range of tasks, including combining text from many cells, extracting certain characters from a text string, and replacing specific letters within a text string. The Excel text functions most frequently used are CONCATENATE, LEFT, and RIGHT.

The CONCATENATE function allows users to combine text from two or more cells into a single cell. When working with large datasets comprising numerous types of information that need to be combined into a single cell, this is extremely useful. One or more comma-separated inputs can be passed to the

CONCATENATE function. Each argument may be a text string, a cell reference, or both.

Users of the LEFT function can take a specific number of characters out of the beginning of a text string. The text string and the required character count are the two inputs accepted by the LEFT function. This comes in particularly convenient when working with text data that follows a set format, such dates or phone numbers. A user can, for example, extract the first three characters of a phone number by using the LEFT function with a value of 3 for the number of characters to extract.

Users of the RIGHT function can take a specific number of characters out of the end of a text string. The text string and the specified character count are the two arguments accepted by the RIGHT function. Working with text data that has a consistent format, like email addresses or file extensions, makes this very useful. For instance, a user can use the RIGHT function with a value of 3 for the number of characters to extract to extract the file extension from a list of file names.

In addition to CONCATENATE, LEFT, and RIGHT, Excel also has MID, LEN, and SUBSTITUTE text functions. Users can extract a specific amount of characters from the middle of a text string using the MID function. The length of a given text string is returned by the LEN function. Users can swap out a specific character or group of characters within a text string for another character or group of characters by using the SUBSTITUTE function.

Text functions can be useful for Excel users who need to handle text data in a variety of ways. Users can create more complex formulas and functions that accurately reflect the data they are working with by combining the CONCATENATE, LEFT, and RIGHT operations with other text functions. Excel is an effective tool for professionals in a range of areas, including finance, accounting, marketing, and sales, thanks to its support for text operations.

Excel's text functions are a crucial tool that give users a variety of options for editing and combining text data. Users can create more complex formulas and functions that accurately reflect the data they are working with by combining the CONCATENATE, LEFT, and RIGHT operations with other text functions. Excel is an effective tool for professionals in a range of areas, including finance, accounting, marketing, and sales, thanks to its support for text operations.

- Date and time functions (TODAY, DATE, NOW)

A key feature of Excel is its date and time functions, which may be used to carry out a number of calculations and manipulations involving dates and times. There are several uses for the built-in date and time functions in Excel, including TODAY, DATE, and NOW.

The function TODAY provides the current date as a result. In a cell, use "=TOday()" to use the TODAY function. The cell holding the formula will then show the current date. Counting the days between two dates and determining an object or person's age are only two of the many uses for TODAY.

Using the year, month, and day, the DATE function creates a date. You must supply distinct parameters for the year, month, and day in order to utilize the DATE function. You might enter "=DATE(2023,1,1)" into a cell to set a date for January 1st, 2023 using the DATE function. After that, the date will be shown in the cell with the formula.

The current date and time are returned by the NOW function. In a cell, type "=NOW()" to use the NOW function. The current date and time will then be shown in the cell that contains the formula. The NOW function can be used for a number of things, like calculating the amount of time left until a deadline or noting the interval between two events.

Excel contains a number of additional functions that can be used to carry out more complex computations in addition to these basic date and time capabilities. The DATEDIF function, for instance, can be used to determine the number of years, months, or days that separate two dates. The EOMONTH function can determine the final day of the month using a specified date. A time based on hours, minutes, and seconds can be created using the TIME function.

You can do complex calculations and make countless changes to data by using Excel's date and time tools. You can design aesthetically beautiful and useful workbooks by mastering date and time functions with practice and knowledge. Excel's date and time features are a powerful tool that may be used for a wide range of tasks, from straightforward calculations to intricate data analysis.

Chapter 5: Data Visualization with PivotTables and PivotCharts

- Understanding PivotTables and PivotCharts

PivotTables and PivotCharts are powerful Excel tools for rapidly and easily analyzing and summarizing massive amounts of data. These tools allow you to see and alter data in a flexible and dynamic manner, allowing you to make informed decisions based on the information you have. PivotTables are used to summarize and aggregate information from several sources. To construct a PivotTable, first choose the data to be analyzed, then click the "Insert" tab and select "PivotTable." Excel will then generate a blank PivotTable for you to personalize to your specifications. Drag and drop the fields you want to examine into the PivotTable fields section to build a PivotTable. The PivotTable can then be used to show and analyze data in a variety of ways, such as summing, average, or counting data.

PivotCharts are used to display information from a PivotTable. To make a PivotChart, first create a PivotTable, then click the "Insert" tab and select "PivotChart." Excel will then generate a graphic using the data from the PivotTable. PivotCharts offer a dynamic approach to view and analyze data by allowing you to modify the chart style, layout, and formatting options with ease.

PivotTables and PivotCharts are excellent tools for analyzing and summarizing massive amounts of data. They are especially beneficial when dealing with complex or difficult-to-understand data. You may quickly and easily spot trends, patterns, and outliers in your data with PivotTables and PivotCharts, and make informed decisions based on the information you have.

Excel has a variety of more complex tools that may be used to further personalize and analyze your data, in addition to basic

PivotTable and PivotChart functionality. You can, for example, utilize the "Slicers" function to filter your data based on certain criteria. You can also utilize the "Grouping" option to categorize your data, such as months or years.

You can quickly and simply analyze and summarize massive sets of data by understanding PivotTables and PivotCharts. Workbooks that are both useful and visually appealing, as well as providing actionable insights and information, can be created with practice and experience. PivotTables and PivotCharts are key Excel tools for making educated decisions and staying ahead of the competition.

- Creating a PivotTable from data

Excel's pivot tables are a helpful tool for quickly summarizing and analyzing enormous amounts of data. A PivotTable may be made in a few easy steps and is a straightforward process. Before you can create a PivotTable, you must have data to analyze. There should be a consistent layout, column headers, and tabular organization for this data. Once you have your data, select any cell within the data range by selecting the Insert tab on the Excel ribbon. The Create PivotTable dialog box will then appear after you choose the PivotTable button.

In the Create PivotTable dialog box, you can decide whether to create your pivot table in a new or existing worksheet. Additionally, you can decide whether to include filters or slicers as well as where to arrange the PivotTable fields. The PivotTable will be built after you click OK after making your selections.

By default, PivotTable will be created in Excel blank, with the PivotTable Field List on the right side of the screen. To choose how you want to summarize and analyze your data, drag and drop fields from your data into the Rows, Columns, Values, and Filters sections of the PivotTable Field List.

Drag the Region field to the Rows area, the Product field to the Columns area, and the Sales Amount field to the Values area if your sales dataset includes columns for Region, Product, and Sales Amount. To give you a consolidated view of your data, Excel will add the Sales Amount for each combination of Region and Product.

PivotTables have several sophisticated options that may be utilized to further personalize and analyze your data in addition to their basic functionality. Calculated fields, for example, can be used to execute calculations on your data within the PivotTable, such as computing a profit margin based on sales and expenses. PivotTable filters and slicers can also be used to dynamically filter and dive down into your data.

Overall, using Excel to create a PivotTable is a simple and powerful approach to evaluate and summarize vast volumes of data. You may quickly gain insights into your data that might be difficult or time-consuming to achieve through manual analysis by following a few simple steps and exploiting some of PivotTables' advanced features.

- Filtering and sorting PivotTable data

An important Excel tool that can be used to rapidly and effectively evaluate and summarize enormous volumes of data is the ability to filter and sort PivotTable data. You may view and alter data in a flexible and dynamic fashion with these tools, enabling you to make decisions based on the facts at hand.

By choosing particular criteria, filtering PivotTable data is used to reduce the results of a PivotTable. You must select the filtering criteria by clicking on the drop-down arrow adjacent to the field you wish to filter before you can begin filtering PivotTable data. You could, for instance, use filtering to just show the sales data for a particular region or product.

To arrange the outcomes of a PivotTable in a particular order, sort PivotTable data. You must select the sort order you wish to employ by clicking on the drop-down arrow adjacent to the field in the PivotTable whose data you want to sort. For instance, you could use sorting to show the sales numbers from top to lowest in descending order.

PivotTable data can be filtered and sorted to provide a powerful means to evaluate and condense enormous sets of data. They are especially helpful when working with complicated or challenging-to-understand data. You can quickly and easily spot trends, patterns, and outliers in your data by utilizing filtering and sorting. Then, you can base your judgments on the knowledge you have.

Excel has a variety of more sophisticated tools in addition to the fundamental filtering and sorting capabilities that may be used to further modify and analyze your data. For instance, you can utilize the "Top 10" function to display the top 10 products according to a particular criterion, such sales numbers. Additionally, you can search for particular items or values in your pivot table using the "Search" option.

You can become an expert at rapidly and effectively evaluating and summing up massive sets of data by mastering filtering and sorting PivotTable data. Workbooks that are useful, visually beautiful, and that offer insights and knowledge that can be put to use can be made with practice. PivotTable data filtering and sorting are crucial Excel capabilities that can aid in decision-making and help you keep one step ahead of the competition.

- Creating a PivotChart from a PivotTable

After establishing a PivotTable, you can rapidly construct a PivotChart in Excel to display and analyze your data visually. A PivotChart, which is effectively a chart built on a PivotTable, allows you to quickly and easily analyse your data in a graphical format.

Before attempting to make a PivotChart from your PivotTable, be sure it is appropriately structured and contains the data you wish to chart. After that, click on any cell in the pivot table to select it, then select the Insert tab from the Excel ribbon. When you click the PivotChart button there, the Create PivotChart dialog box will then show up.

In the Create PivotChart dialog box, you can choose whether to build your pivot chart in a new worksheet or an existing worksheet. A pie chart, column chart, bar chart, or line chart are just a few of the chart types you can choose from. You can produce the PivotChart by clicking OK after making your options.

By default, Excel creates a blank PivotChart and opens the PivotChart Field List on the right side of the screen. Drag and drop the fields from your pivot table into the Axis (Category) and Values sections of the PivotChart Field List to select how you want to plot your data.

To summarize sales data by region and product, for example, you could drag the Region column to the Axis (Category) area and the Sales Amount field to the Values area of a PivotTable. Excel will automatically create a column chart that shows the total sales for each region.

PivotCharts' additional features can be utilized in addition to their core capabilities to further modify and analyze your data. For instance, you may dive deeper into your data and filter it dynamically using PivotChart filters. To alter the design of your chart, you can also use chart formatting options, such as altering the type of chart, adding titles and labels, and changing the colors and styles.

When designing PivotCharts, it's crucial to keep in mind that they are connected to the underlying PivotTable. The PivotChart will automatically update to reflect any changes you make to the PivotTable as a result. For instance, the PivotChart will update to reflect changes if you add a new field to the PivotTable or modify the filter options.

A PivotChart in Excel is a potent tool for visual data exploration and analysis. You may quickly gain insights into your data that might take time or be difficult to achieve through manual analysis by following a few simple steps and utilizing some of the sophisticated features of PivotCharts.

- Customizing PivotTable and PivotChart elements

Excel's ability to customize PivotTable and PivotChart elements enables the creation of aesthetically appealing and instructive data summaries. These tools provide a versatile and dynamic method for viewing and manipulating data, enabling you to make informed decisions based on the knowledge you possess.

Customizing PivotTable elements entails altering the look and functionality of PivotTables to suit your needs. This may involve modifying the PivotTable's layout, adding or removing fields, and modifying the data's formatting. You could, for instance, modify a PivotTable to display subtotals and grand totals for select fields, or to display data in a particular format, such as currency or percentage.

Customizing PivotChart elements entails adjusting PivotCharts' design and behavior to better fit your needs. This may involve modifying the chart type, adding or removing chart elements, and modifying the data presentation. You may, for instance, configure a PivotChart to display data in a specific chart type, such as a bar chart or pie chart, or to display data labels or a legend.

Excel offers a variety of sophisticated tools that may be used to further alter and analyze your data, in addition to its fundamental modification capabilities. Using "Conditional Formatting," for instance, you can emphasize specific data points or trends in your PivotTable or PivotChart. Additionally, you may utilize "Data Validation" to restrict the data that can be inserted into your PivotTable or PivotChart.

By learning the customization of PivotTable and PivotChart elements, you can develop workbooks that are both useful and visually beautiful, and that deliver insights and information that can be put into action. With practice and expertise, you can become adept at customizing PivotTable and PivotChart features to meet your needs and creating data summaries that can be easily comprehended by others.

Excel's key tool for customizing PivotTable and PivotChart features will help you make informed decisions and stay ahead of the competition. By creating visually beautiful and insightful data summaries using these tools, you may obtain a deeper knowledge of your data and make more informed decisions.

Chapter 6: Macros and Automation

- Understanding macros and VBA code

The creation of new functionality and the automation of repetitive tasks are made possible by Excel's macros and VBA (Visual Basic for Applications) code. Excel users can significantly reduce their time and effort by understanding how macros and VBA code work.

A macro is a group of actions that may be performed with a single click after being recorded. Automating repetitive tasks like data preparation and chart production can be done with macros. The Developer tab on Excel's ribbon must first be selected in order to create a macro. Then, after performing the appropriate automated tasks, you can record a macro by selecting the Record Macro button. The macro can then be stored and set to a button or keyboard shortcut for easy access after it has been recorded.

A programming language called VBA allows for the development of original Excel features. VBA code can be used to automate difficult tasks like importing data from outside sources or creating unique processes. Press Alt + F11 or select the Visual Basic button on the Developer tab in Excel to launch the VBA editor.

You can develop custom code that interacts with Excel and other Office apps in the VBA editor. Code written in VBA can be used to construct custom functions, make computations, and alter data, among other things. VBA code can also be used to generate user forms, allowing for the creation of customized user interfaces for Excel spreadsheets.

One of the benefits of using macros and VBA code is that they may be reused and even shared with other users. Macros and VBA code can be saved in a personal macro workbook or a separate add-in file that can be imported into any Excel sheet. However, it is vital to utilize macros and VBA code with caution, as improper use could cause damage to your machine or compromise your data. Always use caution when executing macros or downloading code from untrusted sources, and thoroughly test your code before deploying it in a production environment.

In addition to recording macros and writing VBA code, there are numerous online resources that can assist you in learning more about these advanced Excel features. Microsoft's website contains a lot of documentation and tutorials, and there are numerous online communities and forums where Excel users may ask questions and receive assistance.

Overall, understanding macros and VBA code is a crucial ability for anyone who frequently uses Excel. By automating repetitive operations and developing bespoke functionality, you can save time and optimize your workflow, allowing you to concentrate on more crucial duties.

- Recording a simple macro

When doing repetitive tasks, Excel's ability to record a simple macro could help you save time and effort. A macro is a group of scripted instructions and actions that can be played back to automate a process. Repeated tasks can be automated and finished in a fraction of the time it would take to do them manually by recording a simple macro.

The Developer tab must initially be enabled in order to record a straightforward macro in Excel. This can be done by choosing "Options" from the "File" menu, then "Customize Ribbon." Click "OK" after checking the "Developer" checkbox. You can record a macro by choosing the "Record Macro" button in the "Code" area of the Developer tab after the Developer tab has been enabled.

When you click the "Record Macro" button in Excel, the "Record Macro" dialog box will appear. You may give your macro a name and assign it to a keyboard shortcut or button using this dialog box. Additionally, you can decide whether the macro should be saved in the current worksheet or a new one. You can start recording your actions once you've finished setting up your macro.

When Excel starts recording your actions in "Record Macro" mode, carry out the action you want to automate. For example, you would choose the table and apply the required formatting options to automate the task of formatting the table. Each action you take as part of the macro will be recorded and stored by Excel.

By selecting the "Stop Recording" button in the "Code" part of the "Developer" page, you can end the macro recording. Click "Run" to play the macro back after choosing it from the "Macros" list in the "Code" section of the Developer tab.

You may automate repetitive operations and save time and effort while working with huge data sets by recording simple macros. You can become adept at recording macros and producing usable and efficient workbooks through practice and experience.

Excel's ability to record a simple macro is vital for making educated decisions and staying ahead of the competition. By automating repetitive processes with macros, you can concentrate on more important duties and increase your productivity and efficiency.

- Editing and running macros

If you have already created a macro in Excel, you might need to edit it or run it again. Macro editing and execution can be done easily by using the Visual Basic Editor (VBE).

To open the Visual Basic Editor (VBE), press Alt + F11, or to modify a macro, choose the Visual Basic button on the Developer page. In the VBE, you may navigate to the module that contains your macro and make any necessary code edits there. Once you've finished changing the macro, you can save your changes and leave the VBE.

To start a macro, either set a button or keyboard shortcut to it, or start it directly from the VBE. Simply choose the macro you want to execute from the VBE and press F5 on your keyboard or the Run button. The macro will execute the recorded or programmed actions.

Before modifying and running macros, it's essential to take caution and thoroughly test your code to make sure it works as intended. It's a good idea to make a backup copy of your worksheet before making any changes to the code because even small adjustments can have unintended consequences. There are numerous sophisticated capabilities in Excel that may be used to tweak and expand the functionality of your macros in addition to editing and running macros. For instance, you can build more sophisticated macros that carry out calculations or work with data by using variables and loops. Additionally, you can employ error handling to stop your macros from malfunctioning or crashing in the face of unforeseen circumstances.

Security is a crucial factor to take into account when working with macros. When downloading and using macros from unidentified sources, it's crucial to exercise caution because they could potentially damage your computer or compromise your data if not handled appropriately. Additionally, you should be aware of Excel's security settings, which can be used to regulate which macros are permitted to execute and whether or not the user is prompted before running a macro.

Overall, modifying and using macros is a crucial ability for anyone who frequently uses Excel. You may save time and enhance productivity by using macros to customize and automate your workflow, which will free up your time for other crucial duties. You can master designing and using macros in Excel with a little practice and focus on detail.

- Assigning macros to buttons or keyboard shortcuts

You can save time and effort by using Excel's crucial feature that lets you apply macros to buttons or keyboard shortcuts when doing common tasks. Instead of utilizing the Developer tab or menus, you may quickly and easily execute a macro by assigning it to a button or keyboard shortcut.

Before you can add a macro to a button in Excel, you must first build the button. By clicking the "Insert" tab, selecting "Shapes," and then selecting the form you wish to use as a button, you may make your selection. After creating the button, you can assign the macro to it by right-clicking the button and choosing "Assign Macro" from the context menu.

After selecting the macro you want to associate with the button, click "OK." By clicking the button, the macro can then be executed.

Before you can connect a macro to a key combination in Excel, you must decide which key combination you wish to use. You may then attach the macro to the key combination by clicking the "File" tab, selecting "Options," and then selecting "Customize Ribbon." Then, by selecting "Keyboard Shortcuts" from the drop-down menu, you may select the macro you want to attach from the "Categories" list. By selecting the "Press new shortcut key" field and entering the desired key combination after selecting the macro, you can assign it a key combination. By selecting "Assign," the key combination can then be allocated to the macro.

You can save time and effort while doing repetitive tasks in Excel by assigning macros to buttons or keyboard shortcuts. With enough time and skill, you might be able to develop workbooks that are both useful and efficient by assigning macros to buttons or keyboard commands.

Excel's ability to assign macros to buttons or keyboard shortcuts is a crucial feature that can assist you in staying competitive and making wise decisions. You may focus on more important tasks and increase productivity and efficiency by utilizing macros to automate repetitive processes and assigning them to buttons or keyboard shortcuts.

Chapter 7: Advanced Charting Techniques

- Creating complex charts (e.g. scatter, radar, combo)

There are numerous chart types in Excel that may be used to visualize data in various ways. More complex charts may occasionally be necessary to completely evaluate and comprehend your data, even while straightforward charts like bar charts and line charts are effective for many uses. We'll examine some of Excel's more sophisticated chart types in this section, including scatter charts, radar charts, and combo charts.

One variable is plotted on the x-axis of a scatter chart, and another variable is plotted on the y-axis. When comparing two sets of data to see whether there is a correlation between them, scatter charts can be used to identify trends or patterns in the data. To make a scatter chart in Excel, just select your data and navigate to the Insert tab in the ribbon. The Scatter chart type that best fits your data should be selected.

Radar charts are two-dimensional graphs that show multivariate data. They are often referred to as spider charts or star charts. Radar charts are useful when comparing numerous variables across various categories, such as product characteristics or performance metrics. To create a radar chart, select your data and navigate to the Insert tab in the Excel ribbon. The Radar chart type that best fits your data should be selected.

Multiple chart types are combined onto one graph in combo charts. When displaying multiple data points on a single graph or comparing data from other chart styles, combo charts come in helpful. To create a combination chart, select your data and navigate to the Insert tab in the Excel ribbon. Select the chart types you want to combine, followed by the Combo chart type. When building complicated charts in Excel, it is crucial to take the structure and formatting of your chart into account. To alter the appearance of your chart, you can modify the kind of chart, add or delete chart elements, and alter the colors and styles. To give context and make your chart simpler to understand, you can also add chart titles and labels. There are other sophisticated tools available to further manipulate and analyze your data, in addition to the basic functionality of complex charts. For instance, in a scatter chart, trendlines can be used to show the overall trend of your data, but in a radar chart, data labels can be used to show the values of your data points. Using the chart formatting settings, you may also alter the look of your chart by altering the font size, adding a background color, or modifying the axis scales. Overall, using Excel to create complicated charts is a wonderful method to display and study your data. You can gain insights into your data that would be difficult or time-consuming to achieve through manual analysis by utilizing some of the advanced features of Excel charts. You can make professional-looking charts that effectively communicate your facts to others with a little effort and experimenting.

- Adding secondary axes and trendlines

Using secondary axes and trendlines in Excel can help you obtain a better understanding of your data and detect trends and patterns. You can plot various data sets on the same chart and compare them more readily by adding a secondary axis. You may discover trends in your data and make predictions based on the information you have by adding a trendline.

You must first construct a chart in Excel before you can add a secondary axis. You can do this by selecting the data to be charted and then clicking the "Insert" tab. You can then choose the chart type you want to use, and Excel will generate a chart based on your data. After you've built the chart, you can add a secondary axis by right-clicking on the data series you want to plot on the secondary axis. You may then pick "Format Data Series" and then "Secondary Axis" from the menu. Excel will then insert a secondary axis into the chart and plot the data series on it.

To add a trendline to an Excel chart, first build a chart. You can do this by selecting the data to be charted and then clicking the "Insert" tab. You can then choose the chart type you want to use, and Excel will generate a chart based on your data. After you have built the chart, you can add a trendline to it by choosing the data series and right-clicking on it. You can then choose "Add Trendline" and the type of trendline you want to use. Excel will then add a trendline to the chart and display the trendline's equation.

You can make charts that are more informative and easier to interpret by including supplementary axes and trendlines. You can become competent in adding secondary axes and trendlines to construct charts that provide practical insights and information with practice and experience.

Using secondary axes and trendlines in Excel is an important tool for making educated decisions and staying ahead of the competition. You may obtain a deeper understanding of your data and make better decisions based on the information you have by using these tools to produce charts that are more informative and easier to interpret.

- Customizing chart formatting (e.g. colors, fonts)

To create outstanding Excel graphics, it is essential to customize chart layout. By choosing the right colors, fonts, and styles, you may make your charts more amusing and comprehensible. In this section, we'll examine a few choices for modifying the formatting of your Excel charts.

One of the simplest ways to alter your chart's design is to modify its colors. You can choose one of Excel's many color schemes to fit the look and feel of your data or your company's logo. To change the colors, just select the chart and click the Format option in the Excel ribbon. Then you can choose a different color scheme or make a unique color palette.

Another method to alter the formatting of your chart is to modify the fonts. You can use a variety of font styles in Excel to match the tone of your data or your company's logo. Go to the Format tab on the Excel ribbon and choose your favorite font style to modify the fonts on your chart.

Along with changing the colors and fonts, you may also alter the arrangement and style of your chart's components. To add context and improve your chart's readability, you can, for instance, add or remove chart titles, axis names, and data labels. To make your chart components more aesthetically pleasing, you can also alter their sizes and arrangements. Another critical part of modifying chart style is making sure your chart is available to all users. This includes using easy-to-read colors and fonts and eliminating patterns or components that may cause confusion for individuals with visual impairments. Excel has a number of accessibility options for making your charts more inclusive, such as high contrast mode and screen reader support.

Customizing the formatting of charts in Excel is a critical step in producing successful visualizations. You may make your charts more entertaining and understandable by using the proper colors, fonts, and styles. You can design professional-looking charts that effectively communicate your data to others with a little experimenting and attention to detail.

Chapter 8: Tips and Tricks for Mastering Excel

- Customizing the Quick Access Toolbar and Ribbon

When working with large data sets, Excel's ability to customize the Quick Access Toolbar and Ribbon is a helpful feature that can help you save time and effort. By customizing the Quick Access Toolbar and Ribbon, you may add frequently used commands and tools, making them easy to find and use.

In Excel, select "More Commands" from the drop-down arrow next to the toolbar to customize the Quick Access Toolbar. Press "Add" after choosing the command you want to add to the Quick Access Toolbar. Commands can also be removed by selecting them and then choosing "Uninstall." Click "OK" to save your modifications and reload the Quick Access Toolbar after that.

Excel's Ribbon can be customized by right-clicking on it and selecting "Customize the Ribbon." The tab can then be customized by including or deleting groups and activities as necessary. By selecting the groups and commands to be included in the new tab after clicking "New Tab," you may easily add new tabs. Click "OK" to save your modifications and update the Ribbon after you are done.

You can save time and effort while working with large volumes of data by customizing the Quick Access Toolbar and Ribbon. With practice and knowledge, you may become a master at tailoring the Quick Access Toolbar and Ribbon to your particular requirements and create workbooks that are both efficient and successful.

Excel's Quick Access Toolbar and Ribbon customization is a crucial tool for strategic decision-making and remaining one step ahead of the competition. By adding commonly used commands and tools to the toolbar or ribbon, you may increase your productivity and efficiency while concentrating on more crucial tasks.

In addition to changing the Quick Access Toolbar and Ribbon, Excel provides a number of more sophisticated customization features that can be used to further personalize your workspace. For instance, you can modify Excel's design and features using the "Excel Options" dialog box, or you can use the "Themes" feature to alter the color scheme and font style of your workbooks.

By learning Excel's customization features, you may create workbooks that give essential insights and information while also being both functional and aesthetically pleasing. One of the customization options in Excel that can help you boost your productivity and efficiency while working with large volumes of data is customizing the Quick Access Toolbar and Ribbon.

- Using keyboard shortcuts to save time

When working with big data sets, Excel's strong keyboard shortcut feature can help you save time and effort. Without needing to use the mouse or travel through menus, you may quickly and easily execute frequently used commands and tools by using keyboard shortcuts.

You must first master the keyboard shortcuts for the actions and tools you intend to utilize in order to use keyboard shortcuts in Excel. You can do this by consulting the Excel help files or by looking for a list of keyboard shortcuts online. The commands and tools can be used more quickly and effectively once you have mastered the keyboard shortcuts. In Excel, a few frequently used keyboard shortcuts are as follows:

- Ctrl + C: Copy
- Ctrl + V: Paste

- Ctrl + X: Cut

- Ctrl + Z: Undo

- Ctrl + Y: Redo

- Ctrl + A: Select All

- Ctrl + B: Bold

- Ctrl + U: Underline

- Ctrl + I: Italicize

Using these keyboard shortcuts can help you save time and effort while working with large data sets in Excel. With practice and training, you may become an expert at using keyboard shortcuts to open activities and tools more quickly and efficiently.

In addition to these frequently used keyboard shortcuts, Excel provides a variety of additional, more complicated shortcuts that can be used to boost productivity and efficiency. For instance, clicking Alt + F11 will open the Visual Basic Editor, and pressing Ctrl + Shift + L will toggle the filter on and off. Excel keyboard shortcuts can assist you in creating efficient, useful workbooks that provide knowledge and information that is useful. There are numerous features available in Excel that can help you operate more productively and efficiently when dealing with large amounts of data. One of these features is the use of keyboard shortcuts.

To sum up, knowing how to use Excel's keyboard shortcuts is an essential skill that may help you stay competitive and make wise decisions. By using keyboard shortcuts for frequently used functions and tools in Excel when working with large data sets, you may save time and effort. With practice and patience, you may learn how to employ keyboard shortcuts to create workbooks that are efficient, useful, and provide insightful and informative content.

- Using Excel on mobile devices and the web

Excel may be utilized on a multitude of platforms and devices, including mobile devices and the web, and is a strong tool for data analysis and visualization. In this part, we'll look at a few methods you can interact with your data while on the move using Excel on mobile devices and the web.

On mobile devices, Excel

You can create, edit, and browse Excel spreadsheets on your smartphone or tablet thanks to the Excel mobile app, which is available for iOS and Android devices. Many of the functionality found in Excel's desktop application, such as formulae, charts, and formatting choices, are now available in the mobile app.

Working with data while on the go is one of the benefits of using Excel on a mobile device. Your spreadsheets are accessible from anywhere, and you can quickly update or change your data using a mobile device. You may share your spreadsheets with others through the mobile app, email, or cloud storage services like OneDrive or Dropbox.

Using Excel online

You can also create, edit, and view Excel spreadsheets via your web browser thanks to the Excel web app. Many of the same capabilities found in Excel's desktop application, such as formulae, charts, and formatting choices, are also available in the web app.

The capability of real-time collaboration is one benefit of using Excel on the web. Spreadsheets can be collaborated on and shared with others, with updates and changes being automatically synced across all devices. The web app is an effective tool for remote work and collaboration since it enables you to access your spreadsheets from any device with an internet connection.

It's critical to be aware of the constraints imposed by mobile and web-based platforms when using Excel on either of these platforms. There may be some functional or performance variations between the Excel mobile app and online app even though both offer many of the same capabilities as the Excel desktop program. Working with complicated spreadsheets or data sets could also be more difficult on mobile devices due to their smaller screens and different input techniques.

Overall, working with your data on the road and collaborating with others in real-time can be a lot of fun using Excel on mobile devices and the web. You can become skilled in using

Excel on these platforms with some practice and close attention to detail, which will advance your data analysis and visualization skills.

- Finding and using Excel add-ins

The functionality and capabilities of Excel can be expanded by installing add-ins, which are third-party tools or programs. The usage of add-ins is possible for a variety of functions, including data analysis, charting, reporting, and more. We will look at some of the methods in this section for finding and utilizing Excel add-ins to improve data analysis and visualization.

How to Find Excel Add-Ins

There are many sources to find Excel add-ins, including third-party websites, the Microsoft AppSource, and the Excel Add-Ins Store. You can find these add-ins by performing a web search for them or by going to the Insert tab on the Excel ribbon and choosing the Get Add-ins option.

It's crucial to exercise caution and only download add-ins from reliable sources when searching for add-ins. Some add-ins might have malicious software or other bad code that could harm your computer or data. Furthermore, some add-ins might not function as intended or might not be compatible with your version of Excel.

Excel Add-Ins Use

Once an Excel add-in has been downloaded and set up, you may access its features and functionality from the Add-Ins tab or Excel ribbon. Depending on their individual use case, add-ins may offer functionality like new chart kinds, data analysis tools, or reporting templates.

The Solver add-in, which is used for difficult issue analysis and optimization, is a well-known example of an Excel add-in. Using a range of optimization techniques, the Solver add-in enables you to set up and solve optimization issues in Excel, such as determining the ideal production plan or inventory level.

The Power Query add-in, which is used for data analysis and manipulation, is another illustration of an Excel add-in. You may load data from a variety of sources, including databases, websites, and spreadsheets, into Excel for additional analysis with the Power Query add-in.

It's critical to understand the exact features and capabilities of Excel add-ins, as well as any restrictions or dependencies they could have, before using them. Some add-ins could need extra software or data sources to work effectively, while others might have special Excel compatibility requirements.

In general, Excel add-ins can be a potent tool to increase your data analysis and visualization capabilities while also extending the functionality of Excel. You can save time and streamline your workflow, freeing up your attention for other crucial activities, by locating and utilizing the appropriate add-ins for your unique use case. You may improve your skills with Excel add-ins and advance your data analysis and visualization with a little study and practice.

- Troubleshooting common Excel errors

Excel is a potent tool for working with massive data sets, but it is not devoid of difficulties. When dealing with formulas, formatting, or data validation, common Excel problems can arise, which can be irritating and time-consuming to resolve. Here are some troubleshooting tips for typical Excel errors:

An inaccuracy in a formula is one of the most prevalent Excel errors. If you see a #VALUE! or #REF! error, it is possible that the formula is incorrect. Check your formula to ensure that all cell references are accurate and that you're employing the proper syntax.

Check your formatting: formatting errors are another typical Excel issue. If you get a #NUM! or #NAME? issue, the wrong formatting may be to blame. Ensure that you are using the correct number format or text format by examining your formatting.

Verify your data validation Data validation is a great tool for regulating the inputs in your Excel worksheet, but if not configured correctly, it might lead to mistakes. If you see a #N/A or #DIV/0! error, it could be due to a data validation problem. Verify that your data validation configuration is proper.

Excel employs cell references to bind cells together, however these references can sometimes become erroneous or damaged. If you see a #REF! error, the reference to the cell may be erroneous. Check your references to ensure they are accurate and that the cells they link to are still present.

Examine your data. Data problems might be the most hardest to diagnose, but they can also be the most crucial. If you see a #NAME? or #VALUE! problem, it could be due to a data error. Verify that your data is complete and accurate, with no missing values or inaccurate entries.

By following these recommendations, you can avoid the aggravation and time-consuming process of locating and repairing frequent Excel problems. You can become adept at diagnosing Excel issues and creating effective, error-free spreadsheets via practice and experience.

In addition to these ideas, Excel provides a variety of built-in tools for troubleshooting frequent mistakes. For instance, the "Error Checking" tool can be used to identify and repair errors in your worksheet, but the "Track Error" option can be used to trace the source of an error and determine its underlying cause.

By mastering the tools and techniques for diagnosing common Excel issues, you can produce functional, efficient, and actionable workbooks. Excel's ability to troubleshoot common problems is only one of several tools that can increase your productivity and efficiency while working with massive data sets.

Chapter 9: Step-by-Step Examples

Example 1: Creating a Basic Budget Spreadsheet

Basic budget spreadsheets are typically made in Excel, which is also a useful tool for managing finances and keeping track of expenses. In this example, we'll look at how to use Excel's basic calculations and formatting to create a simple budget spreadsheet.

an additional worksheet in Step 1.

To build a new budget spreadsheet in Excel, open a new workbook and create a new worksheet. Include sections like income, expenses, and savings in the worksheet's first row.

Step 2: Add your income and expenses

Next, fill in the appropriate fields with your revenue and spending information. For instance, you might put your rent or mortgage payment in the "expenses" column and your monthly income in the "income" column.

Calculate totals and balances in step three. Employing Formulas

To calculate the overall income, spending, and savings, enter formulas in the corresponding boxes. For instance, you can calculate your total revenue and expenses using the SUM function, and then calculate your monthly savings by subtracting your total expenses from your total income.

Formatting Spreadsheet of yours

To make your budget spreadsheet easier to read and understand, format it using colors, fonts, and styles. To draw attention to important information, use bold or italic typefaces. You can also use color to distinguish between different expense categories.

Maintain and update your spreadsheet.

When you've finished creating your budget spreadsheet, make sure to save it and keep it updated often to account for any changes in your income and outgoings. The spreadsheet can also be used to track your progress over time and pinpoint areas where you could cut costs or increase your savings.

A budget spreadsheet's advanced features can be utilized to further change and analyze your data in addition to its core capabilities. For instance, using charts and graphs, you can display your data and identify trends or patterns. You may also use advanced techniques like VLOOKUP to compare your actual spending with your projected expenses and conditional formatting to highlight data that meets specified criteria.

Making a simple Excel budget spreadsheet is a useful tool for handling money and keeping track of expenses. With a little experience and attention to detail, you can create a spreadsheet that conveys your financial situation clearly and helps you make well-informed financial decisions.

Example 2: Analyzing Sales Data with PivotTables

Excel's PivotTables are a useful tool for analyzing sales data, allowing you to summarize and analyze massive data sets quickly and effectively. In this example, we will utilize PivotTables to examine sales data from a fictitious company in order to acquire insights into their sales success.

To begin, a dataset containing information about sales transactions is required. In this example, we have a dataset with columns for the sale date, the product sold, the quantity sold, and the sale's total revenue.

To generate a PivotTable, we must first pick the data for analysis. This can be accomplished by clicking on any cell within the dataset, then selecting "PivotTable" from the "Insert" menu. Then, we can choose the range of cells we wish to use for the pivot table and click "OK."

Once the PivotTable has been generated, we can begin evaluating the data. For instance, the PivotTable may be used to see which products are selling the most. To accomplish this, we can drag the "Product" column to the "Rows" section and the "Total Revenue" column to the "Values" section. Excel will then construct a table displaying each product's total income.

The PivotTable can also be used to analyze sales trends over time. This can be accomplished by dragging the "Date" field to the "Columns" section and the "Total Revenue" column to the "Values" area. Excel will then build a table that displays the monthly revenue totals.

PivotTables' ability to filter and sort data is an additional helpful function. For instance, we can utilize the PivotTable to determine which products are most popular in a specific location. To accomplish this, we can drag the "Region" field to the "Filters" section and then pick the region for analysis. Then, we may sort the data by total revenue to see which products in that region generate the most profit.

By analyzing sales data with PivotTables, we may get insights into our sales performance and pinpoint areas for improvement. With practice and expertise, we can become adept at utilizing PivotTables to generate useful and actionable reports that can assist us in making more informed business decisions.

In addition to PivotTables, Excel offers a variety of other data analysis tools, including charts and graphs, conditional formatting, and data validation. By understanding these tools and strategies, we can produce workbooks that are both functional and efficient, and that yield insights and information that can be put into action. The ability to analyze sales data with PivotTables is just one of the numerous Excel capabilities that can increase our productivity and efficiency when working with enormous data sets.

Example 3: Using Conditional Formatting to Highlight Data

With the help of Excel's powerful conditional formatting function, you may highlight certain data based on predetermined standards or conditions. In this example, we'll see how to use conditional formatting to highlight particular data in a spreadsheet to make it easier to read and understand.

Select the Data for Step 1 Highlighting

To use conditional formatting, you must first select the data that you want to emphasize. This could be an entire column or row, a collection of cells, or just one cell.

In Step 2, pick a conditional formatting rule.

Choose a conditional formatting rule that adheres to the criteria you wish to stress next. For instance, you might wish to highlight every cell with a particular value, such as every cell that is below or above a certain range.

Excel features conditional formatting rules that can be used to highlight data based on a variety of factors, including data bars, color scales, and icon sets. Step 3: Personalize the Formatting Options

You can change the formatting options after choosing a conditional formatting rule to suit your preferences. For example, you can select the color of the highlight, the width of the data bars, or the type of icon to be used in the icon collection.

You also have the choice of applying multiple conditional formatting rules to the same data to highlight different types of data based on various criteria.

In Step 4, use the Conditional Formatting Rule.

To apply the conditional formatting rule to the data you've chosen, select the formatting options, then click "OK."

After applying conditional formatting, the data will update instantly as it changes, making it simple to track changes and identify trends over time.

Using conditional formatting, you may highlight data in a spreadsheet in a number of different ways. You can use conditional formatting to highlight cells that have mistakes, are above or below a certain threshold, or fulfill a specific set of criteria, such as a specific date or text string, for example.

Overall, conditional formatting can be used in Excel to highlight data and make it easier to read and understand. With a little practice and experimentation, you can master conditional formatting and improve your data analysis and visualization.

Example 4: Creating a Gantt Chart for Project Planning

An effective Excel feature for project planning is the ability to create Gantt charts. In this example, we'll use Excel to make a Gantt chart for a made-up project so that we can learn more about the project's timeframe and resource usage.

We require a dataset with details on the project tasks and their length before we can begin. In this illustration, the task name, start date, duration, and resource used for the activity are all listed in separate columns in the dataset.

We first need to format the data in a particular way before we can generate a Gantt chart. The task name, start date, end date, and resource assigned to the task must all appear in the first column. Then, after choosing the information for the Gantt chart, we may click the "Insert" tab, choose "Bar Chart," and then "Stacked Bar Chart." The columns and rows can then be switched by selecting the stacked bar chart and clicking "Switch Row/Column."

We can begin the data analysis once the Gantt chart has been made. The Gantt chart can be used to determine which tasks are taking the longest and what resources have been allocated to each activity. The Gantt chart, for instance, can be used to determine which tasks are essential to the project's deadline and which resources are over-allocated.

The Gantt chart can be used to change the project timeframe as well. For instance, we can adjust the bar to the right to represent the new end date if a task is taking longer than anticipated. By creating a new row and providing the task name, start date, length, and resource assigned to the task, we can easily add new tasks to the Gantt chart.

The Gantt chart's ability to filter and sort data is another helpful feature. The Gantt chart, for instance, can be used to determine which tasks are allocated to a specific resource. To accomplish this, we can choose the resource we wish to investigate using the filter function. The tasks that are consuming the most time for that resource can then be determined by sorting the data by duration.

We can acquire insights into the project timetable and resource allocation as well as pinpoint areas for improvement by using a Gantt chart for project planning. With training and experience, we can master the creation and application of Gantt charts to produce insightful and useful reports that can aid in the improvement of our business decisions.

Excel offers a variety of other project planning tools in addition to Gantt charts, including timelines, calendars, and project management templates. We can produce workbooks that are effective and practical and that offer insights and knowledge that can be put to use by mastering these tools and processes. One of the numerous capabilities of Excel that can increase productivity and efficiency when working with big data sets is the ability to create Gantt charts for project planning.

Example 5: Building a Loan Amortization Schedule

Making a loan amortization schedule is a common task in finance, and Excel makes it easy to do so. The periodic payments of a loan, the percentage of each payment devoted to interest and principle, and the loan balance following each payment are all shown in a table known as an amortization schedule. We'll examine how to establish an Excel loan amortization schedule in this example.

Step 1: Gather loan information

To develop an amortization schedule, you must collect information about the loan, such as the principle amount, the interest rate, and the length of the loan. The frequency of payments, which may be weekly, bimonthly, or monthly, is something else you should be aware of.

Create the spreadsheet in step two.

By beginning a new spreadsheet in Excel and include the columns for the payment number, payment date, payment amount, interest paid, principle paid, and remaining balance, you may create a table. The payment amount denotes the entire payment, the interest paid denotes the portion applied to interest, the principal paid denotes the fraction applied to principal, and the remaining balance denotes the amount of the loan that is still outstanding after each payment.

Calculate the payment amount in step three.

The payment amount should be calculated using Excel's PMT function. The PMT function establishes the periodic payment for a loan based on the interest rate, the number of payments, and the principle amount. For example, the following formula might be used to calculate the monthly payment for a loan of $100,000 with a term of 30 years and an interest rate of 5%: $536.82 is equal to PMT(5%/12,30*12,100000).

Determine the principal and interest paid in step 4

Calculate the interest and principal paid for each payment using Excel's IPMT and PPMT functions. While the IPMT function calculates the interest paid for a certain payment, the PPMT function calculates the principal paid for a specific payment. For illustration, the following formula might be used to calculate the interest on the initial payment of a loan with a $536.82 monthly payment and a 5% annual interest rate:=IPMT(5%)/12,1,30*12,100000 = $416.67. The first payment's principle would be determined as follows:

=PPMT(5%/12,1,30*12,100000) = $120.15.

Step 5: Determine the Outstanding Balance

After each payment, deduct the principle paid from the prior total to get the loan's remaining balance. For instance, if your loan has a total of $100,000 and your monthly payment is $536.82, you may use the formula below to determine how much is still owed after the first payment: =$100,000-$120.15 = $99,879.85.

Step 6: Fill in the Table

After determining the first payment's payment amount, interest and principal paid, and remaining balance, you may complete the table by copying the formulas down the columns for the subsequent payments.

In conclusion, creating an Excel loan amortization schedule is a strong tool for managing your debts and keeping track of your payments. You can develop a professional-looking spreadsheet that successfully communicates your loan information and supports your financial decision-making with a little experience and attention to detail.

Printed in Great Britain
by Amazon

26343667R00057